WHAT GOES ON IN THIS HOUSE

Some Secrets Were Never Meant to Be Kept

ANISSA D. JONES

WHAT GOES ON IN THIS HOUSE by Anissa D. Jones
Published by Empoword Publishing Worldwide
Copyright © 2025 by Anissa D. Jones
What Goes On in This House: Some Secrets Were Never Meant to Be Kept
by Anissa D. Jones

Printed in the United States of America. All rights reserved solely by the author. The author guarantees all artwork and contents are original and do not infringe upon the legal rights of any other person, entity, or work. The author further guarantees that any content that is not original is rightfully and truthfully cited to the best of the author's knowledge. No part of this book may be reproduced, stored in a retrieval system, or transmitted in any form without the permission of Empoword Publishing Worldwide and the author. The views expressed in this book are not necessarily those of the publisher.

Empoword Publishing Worldwide
17127 Wax Rd Bldg A
Greenwell Springs, LA 70739
www.EmpowordPublishing.com
(225) 412-3130

The cover has been designed by Danshelle Jones located in Los Angeles, CA gemintelligenceagency@gmail.com.

This book is protected by the copyright laws of the United States of America. The scanning, uploading, and distribution of this book or any part thereof via the Internet or any other means without the permission of the publisher or author is illegal and punishable by law. Permission will be granted upon request. Please purchase only authorized editions and do not participate in or encourage the electronic piracy of copyrighted materials.

This book recounts certain events in the life of Anissa D. Jones according to the best of the author's recollection and perspective. While all stories are true, the author has, to the best of her ability, changed some names and identifying details to protect the privacy of those involved.

The purpose of this book is to entertain, motivate, and inspire the reader. The author and publisher shall have neither liability or responsibility for anyone(s) with respect to any loss or damage caused, directly or indirectly, by the information contained in this book. Unless otherwise noted, all scriptures referenced in this book are in The Holy Bible New King James Version Copyright © 1982 Thomas Nelson, Inc., Publishers.

Paperback ISBN: 979-8-9945120-0-5
eBook ISBN: 979-8-9945120-1-2

ACKNOWLEDGEMENTS

I would like to thank my Father, John Henry Jones, Sr, may his soul rest in peace. My daughter-in-law, Sarah Jones, and my granddaughter whom I never had the opportunity to meet, Anyssa Roxanne Jones. To all my beautiful children, Darique, Danshelle, David, Dinah, Judah, Hannah, and Stephen. I thank my friends for asking me about this book and pushing me to complete it. Special thanks to Prophet Stephen Chestnut and Elizabeth Lawson. I thank my editor and publisher because she did not rush me to complete my assignment but understood the Kairos moment in which it was to happen. Most of all I thank God for sending Jesus to rescue me, heal me, and deliver me, and the Holy Spirit for guiding me, never leaving my side.

TABLE OF CONTENTS

Introduction 7

Chapter 1 The Beginning 10

Chapter 2 The Brokenness 34

Chapter 3 The Identity Struggle 51

Chapter 4 The Liberation 65

Chapter 5 The Journey To Wholeness 71

Call To Salvation 74

About The Author 76

Go Follow Anissa! 77

Introduction

I wrote this book because, for years as an African American woman, I was told time and time again this old age mantra that says, "what goes on in this house, stays in this house!" After hearing it repeatedly, I believed it. It was a lie. In fact, this lie was used to cover much of the turmoil that existed in my own family. Issues like incest, addictions, deep family secrets, perversion, and lust ran rampant for years. For decades, my family and I covered tons of secrets with the hope of hiding our dysfunction.

Some families undergo extensive counseling after tumultuous experiences. Our family never experienced counseling, healing or deliverance, and as a result, we lacked identity, and began to embody the lies we have believed about our trauma.

However, now it is time to tell what happened in our dysfunctional home. I tell this story, not to broadcast my life or demean or degrade my family, but to set others free. It is my hope to encourage those who have experienced deep pain, to let them know that there is life on the other side of the pain and grief. Just as God helped me and is helping me to be free, He can and will do the same for you. Healing, freedom, wholeness and restoration are possible for you. Your life does not have to remain the way it has always been. I wanted better and I know you do too. You deserve better. You do not have to live in shame and fear any longer.

God forgives you, now it is time to forgive yourself. No longer will you worry about your family or friends or what they think. You will speak the truth for your freedom.

Like me, I know you have held these secrets in for so long that you never thought it would be possible to talk about them. You have carried the guilt and shame and maybe even passed it on to your children. This book is for you. We need your voice. I am here to help you on your journey to freedom no matter what you have been through. The declaration, 'what goes on in this house, stays in this house' has been a prison cell for you. If you have experienced rape, molestation, incest, being seen as "fast," feeling inadequate or unloved, that is not who you are. These labels do not define who you are or who you are becoming.

What happened to you made you a prisoner and I want you to get your voice back and enjoy life the way it was meant to be lived. You deserved better and God intended better for you. I love you, let's do this together.

In this book, I tell my story, but let's use it to create a safe space to go back, think about what happened, and explore why it is not your fault and never has been. Some of you have buried it so far down that it might hurt to recall it, but it is okay. The weight of the secret has burdened you down. That secret is too heavy for you to carry. It is time to put it down. It is time to release it. It is time you know the truth about who you really are. The truth is: You are loved!

You are important! You are worthy! You are special! You are beautiful! You are smart! You are strong! You are God's son; you are God's daughter! He loves you deeply!

CHAPTER 1
The Beginning

GROWING UP

One night, I went to school, practiced, came home, did my homework, took care of my son, and cleaned the kitchen. I had just laid down in bed when my mom asked me for some water. My sister was laying right beside her. Because of my sister's proximity to her, I thought, "You have got to be kidding me." It was true, mom wanted me to get her water despite my sister's closeness. Well, good thing for me, I had just made a cup of water for myself, so I took it into her room. Eager to pounce, my sister said, "Mom doesn't drink out of plastic cups." I discarded my sister's words and handed the cup to mom. With the quickness, mom handed the cup back to me. So, I went to go get her a glass of water instead. Once I made it to the kitchen, I dumped the same water from the cup into a glass. My sister was still monitoring my every move. This time she let me know that mom would need ice in her glass because she would not drink warm water. Again, I ignored my sister's taunts and continued towards my mom. Within seconds, she sent me back into the kitchen to get the ice and warned me to stop making so much noise as I rustled around in the kitchen and threatened to spank me. I was 15 years old. As Murphy's Law would have it, as soon as I opened the fridge, tons of items fell to the floor. Mom rushed down the hall with a belt aimed directly at me. A tussle ensued. I weighed only 125 pounds and though mom was much bigger, I stood my ground. I had made up in my mind that I was not going to get beat for this foolishness that my able-bodied sister had instigated. Mom swung at me with the belt, and I caught it with my right hand. We fought over the belt until I fell to the ground, and she put her foot on me. I was determined not to get beat that day, and I didn't. I will never forget this moment, in fact, it was the last time she ever tried to beat me again.

I am the oldest of four children. I have two sisters and a brother. My mom, dad, and sisters lived at my grandparents' house, next to my grandpa's brother's house for my first four years. Until I was age five, living next to my cousins was cool. My aunt was a medicine woman of sorts. If any of us experienced any ailments, she would cure us with one of her natural remedies. My grandparents lived in Maryland as the caretakers of an estate. We visited them occasionally and they came home various times of the year as well.

The estate had everything, a pool, gas station, multiple cars, houses, and ponds. Mom and dad bought a house when I was 5 so we moved from the estate. Even after our move to our own house, I still spent a lot of time at my grandma's house. One of my uncles was like my big brother. I never realized we were so close in age until he passed away many years later. All I knew is that he was the coolest person to hang around. My uncle and I played basketball and card games. I hated when we played, hot hands or pinochle. He would always win and tear my hands and knuckles up. We would take walks to our great-grandma's house down the street, watch cartoons every Saturday morning together and then wrestle. Once I got to high school, the only reason I could go to dances was because my uncle agreed to take me.

After we moved into our new house I made a new best friend. She did not like me at first but later, she became my best buddy. She could come over to my house and I could go over to hers. We played together all the time. Spades, jack rocks, hand games, board games, dancing, singing, you name it we did it. She had an older brother who was FINE! My bestie's house was a great escape for me. I had more freedom and liberty at her house than mine. There I could enjoy just being a kid, boys could come over and I could listen to music. We spent most of our days together, especially during the summer. As teenagers, we used to go to parties together. I loved to dance and listen to music. I lived in front of the record player, the radio, and the television.

Once my mom's third daughter arrived, I fed her, changed her, and carried her around on my hip. I was on big sister duty all the time. She was my real-life doll baby. I was six when she was born. All of my mother's daughters are three years apart. My brother is only two years apart from my youngest sister. As my younger sister got older, all three girls were put in one room sleeping in one bed, and my brother had a room all to himself. I was a little disgruntled. When we got new beds, I had my bed and my sisters had bunk beds. We all got along well as little kids.

As I recall my childhood, I do not remember a lot during the ages from six to eight years old. It was during this time that I was being molested by one of my cousins (more on this later) By age 10, I could cook, clean, iron, and do laundry. I was a latchkey kid who watched my brother and sisters. They were 7, 4, and a baby. I was the mom when my parents were away. I fed them, I made and cleaned bottles, fixed formulas, did chores and I could spank them with a belt if they did not listen. I was always mature for my age and very smart and intuitive. I guess this came with being the oldest. During summer breaks, because our parents made too much money to qualify for the fun summer camp that most of my friends were able to go to, I was stuck at home. They went on fun field trips and got to see their friends all summer long. The good thing was, once my parents were home, they coached softball teams. We used to ride around our neighborhood to pick up kids who were a part of the team. They hopped on the back of my dad's pickup truck or in my mom's Impala. Seat belts were not mandatory, so we were able to fit a crowd of people into the back sit with no problem. Our team was called the *Angels*, we had tons of fun together. The team was made up of neighborhood kids from *New Kent County* as well as some of my cousins. We played against local teams from *New Kent* and *Charles City*. My parents coached our youth team and a team of teenagers as well. All the cute boys were on that team, so I did not mind hanging out at the field. When I was not playing or watching the games I was helping with the concession stand. Hot dogs or hamburgers fresh off the grill were always a treat for us kids.

My dad played softball too. His team was called the *Eagles.* We traveled a lot to games. Some places seemed far away as a kid, but I did not mind the ride. My mom used to dress me and my sister alike when we were little. Everywhere we went, people used to ask if we were twins. My nickname was after a twin from a very popular television show at that time so they would call her *Jody* which was the other twin's name.

We were always well dressed, and our hair neatly done. Mom always kept plenty of options for clothes and things to ensure that we were clean. She also would cook before we left and have it all packaged up for our trip. It was nothing for us to have lunch meat, a loaf of bread, fried chicken, potato salad, deviled eggs, sodas, and snacks in the trunk of the car.

Mom was an amazing cook. Her food was seasoned well, and we loved to eat. She was a great baker. She taught me to make lemon meringue pie. This was no easy task. Yet, I vividly recall a time when mom stopped doing most of the cooking.

Instead of cooking every day, she cooked only on Sundays and Thursdays. My mom was off work these days. At that point, my dad and I took on the other days. We did the cooking except Friday and Saturday nights. They were noted as *fend-for-yourself* nights. During these times we often ate hot dogs, hamburgers, sandwiches, or cheap meals like scrambled eggs, pork and beans, fried bologna with tomato or grilled cheese sandwiches. I loved to eat, so it was then that I began to experiment with different recipes. *Betty Crocker* became my best friend. I kept her cookbooks and index card recipe library close.

My dad enjoyed trying my new meals as well. They mostly came out pretty good. In hindsight, he may have just been happy to get a meal in the first place.

As we grew from teenagers into young adults, things began to shift in my family. It became a very weird dynamic. Our family had this unspoken rule: If I was close to one sister, I could not be close to the other. It is like something would happen to keep us separated. At these times, I could not even be close to my parents. I often found myself taking on the burden of whatever I was told by my siblings. Lies were at work in our family.

If there was a good relationship going on between two of us, it was as if a spirit would jump in and cause jealousy and strife and friction between us. Then, it would switch, the two close sisters then were at odds with each other. At times, even with my parents, somehow, I would think that my mom said something negative about me. And this could cause me to hold a grudge against her. However, the situation was not a reality. Whenever my siblings said something, it would cause this strife and division to come to our family. Later in life this led to my one sister going through seasons where she did not want to be bothered and just stay away.

She would not come to family functions and kept her children away too. I love her children very much, but these instances often put a strain on my relationship with my nieces and nephews. Despite all of this, I always knew that God had the power to heal and restore my family.

One year, over the Christmas holiday, my mom's siblings joined us for Christmas brunch. All my mom's sisters and brothers sat around and reminisced about old times. However, it was interesting to hear them talk because some of the same issues they experienced were happening in my own family.

I remember one conversation where my uncles and aunts thought their parents had favorites and treated their sisters and brothers differently. It turns out, as a kid my mom would get blamed for stuff that one of my aunts did. Another aunt had more liberty and went to school events, and dances. Yet, none of her siblings were able to experience any of these freedoms. Even with my siblings, it was like there existed a silent competition. If you do for one sister, she felt the need to repay it instead of just receiving it. When you try to compliment her, she would make excuses, downing herself. It was all a false humility.

That holiday I learned that the family curses run much deeper than I imagined. At a different time, I listened to my dad talk to his brother and the same foolishness was happening in his family.

Family is meant to be a place of strength and unity. However, in my family, I experienced much division. Some of the family use Christianity as an excuse to exclude other family members, pointing out their sins. I knew that this was not Christlike. Jesus' way was just the opposite. He says, in Jeremiah 31:3   by my lovingkindness, I have drawn thee. I soon learned that the spirit of rejection and the orphan spirit were in operation within my members of my family.

This is my story. These were my beginnings.

———————————

DADDY, DADDY

I want my Daddy

A Father's Love
A father loves, he protects,
He encourages, he covers,
He rebukes, he builds, he
nurtures, he affirms, he
Loves

His love knows no bounds.
His love ignites a flame in you
He knows the real you and loves you in spite of
your past
He sees YOU.
How could he see?
Why does he want to?
You're a daughter.
You are his daughter.

You are loved.
You are successful.
You will finish.
You will finish strong.
You will multiply.
You are great.

You are victorious.
You are free.
TOTALLY FREE.
FINALLY, FREE.

Written By: Anissa D. Jones

———————————

My dad is a great man. He had a servant's heart. He was an amazing teacher and student of God's Word. He was from the Baby Boomer generation. This era showed their love by being providers to their families. Many Baby boomer men expressed their love by coming home every night, putting their checks on the table and providing the basic necessities for their families. Men from their generation rarely verbalized their love, it was only expressed in their actions.

In my house, my mom was the leader. Whatever she said was law. While my dad lived in our home, his presence felt more like an absence.

At times, his lack of a dominant presence caused me to experience feelings of abandonment. When I was little, dad stayed busy. He would spend much of his time engaging with others. Either he was playing softball, working on other cars, or helping someone else, dad was occupied. For as young as I can remember, dad had a good heart. He always wanted to help others and invited them to our home often. While working for *Anheuser Busch*, dad had tons of perks. Some included being gifted cases of beer. These free drinks often made a way for our home to become the party house.

There were countless nights of card parties and drinking parties, we were the party headquarters. Dad used to let me sip on his beer sometimes, *Schlitz Malt Liquor Bull*. When he was not home, I used to steal a few beers to indulge myself. He was a smoker too. Mom did not drink or smoke.

When I was fourteen, my dad got saved. He made Jesus his Lord and savior. His choice changed my world too.

My house was already strict because of my mom and her standards. Yet, dad's salvation had an even greater impact on our household. Our lifestyle became stricter, so much so that we were no longer allowed to play cards.

Things shifted from getting rides from others to make it to church to church becoming our second home. Because I was an athlete, I was sure to join any and every sports team so I could skip church services whenever it was possible.

WHAT DO YOU MEAN I'M PREGNANT?

I was fourteen years old when I became pregnant. My life as a kid was over. I will never forget that day. I was in Mr. Bush's biology class, and I realized I had to keep using the bathroom. I thought maybe I had a bladder infection. I told my mom about it once I got home.

She made me a doctor's appointment. The doctor asked me if I was sexually active. I said no because I thought that meant someone who had sex all the time. I did not know it meant if you have sex at all.

My parents gave me the silent treatment once the doctor called with the results. And to top this news, I was unsure of who the father of my child was. It was between two individuals. One was a white guy who went to my school. We had engaged in sex while at a track meet in broad daylight.

The other person was a black guy from my neighborhood that I had secretly hooked up with once and he prematurely ejaculated. Honestly, I did not count this last instance as sex, but I did not believe I could get pregnant without being penetrated. I just needed to discover how far along I was to know which boy would be the father of my child.

No matter who the dad was, my father was deeply disappointed in me. I was just as shocked as he was. There I was, a kid having a kid. I was in utter disbelief. How did this happen to me?!

Once my son was born, it seemed as if he took my place in my dad's heart. It was like I lost my dad once again. Life was changing for me. I was a kid with adult responsibilities. On one hand, I was reminded by the adults to stay in my place and not get into grown folks' business. On the other hand, I was doing things like going to social services to get services for my son. I filled out these forms to gain benefits, as an adult for my son. It was a very confusing time for me.

It seemed as if the older I became, the less my dad was involved in my life. It was a time when I needed him the most, especially to help me navigate relationships with men.

Dad rarely showed up at my softball/basketball games, track meets, pageants, and award ceremonies anymore. Despite this fact my mom, my aunt and sometimes my grandma remained constant supporters. I could only count on dad to show up and support me if the event was church-related. I did not think about it then, but dad's absence affected me greatly. I saw other girls with their dads. They seemed to have loving and supportive dads, but this was the opposite of my story. Growing up in this environment created a gaping hole in my heart. I longed for love, attention, and affection.

Instead of finding the love I so desired, I found lust, abandonment, and rejection in all the wrong places. I used illegitimate sources like men, sex, alcohol, and food to fulfill that legitimate need. At some points, I even used them all at the same time to cope. My dad did not affirm me. I did not feel loved. I did not feel protected. I did not receive instructions from my father. Because I did not feel the love and support that I not only wanted but needed, men and boys knew exactly what to say because my ears were itching to hear even the slightest compliment. I was attracted to them like bees to honey. I lacked confidence in who I was, and who God created me to be.

Since I did not know who I was, people in the world constantly told me who they thought I was, or who they wanted me to be. I took their advice and complied with whatever they thought I should be. I felt unlovable like something was wrong with me. It affected the way I saw God as Father and how I interacted with him too. Often, I contemplated my true relationship with God. Does God love me? Does God care about me? Why does God allow me to keep going through this?

Years later, I still did not realize that God loved me and has always wanted His best for me. The lies from people and the ones in my mind blocked me from seeing, believing, and trusting in God.

I thought God was a liar just like every other man who had lied to me or rejected me after using me. It was bad.

My household was not affectionate. We did not give or get hugs and kisses. I wanted them, so I searched for them, longed for them, no matter what the cost. A one-night stand, a quickie somewhere with some random person that I just met, and all other sex-driven relationships that I engaged in still left that hole open. I later realized that only God, who is a loving Father, can heal that wound from my earthly father.

Even as an adult, this continued to affect my relationships.

I did not trust people. I often felt they always had an ulterior motive in their exchanges with me. In most instances I was correct. I did not realize that my reckless behavior was more spiritual than it was natural. People were attracted to the broken spaces within me. I longed for love, but attracted lust until my spirit was made whole.

Once I became whole, I realized the need for forgiveness. If you have experienced anything similar, it is important to forgive your father and mother. Once this happens you can love them and ask God to heal you and you can forgive yourself.

Self-forgiveness is the key to breaking cycles. Once you know you are worthy of genuine love and affection, you will attract pure relationships. Otherwise, you will continue cycles of sick behavior in which you are attracted to dysfunctional relationships that you know will not work and that will always leave you empty.

Fast forward to 2019, dad began to have some challenges with his health. My sisters and I attended appointments with him and mom to make sure we were getting all the information and asking all the right questions. 2020, arrived and the pandemic came with it. It was that year my dad was diagnosed with bladder cancer.

The Lord told me to resign from my good government job, and I did. It freed my time up to be available to my family. I was blessed to be able to assist him and mom with caretaking at that time. I did tons of crying while staying at my childhood home during this time. I constantly replayed some of the old memories, but I am grateful to God for the new. Things were not like they were when I was younger. I know now that my daddy loves me, and I felt the love and affection that was missing when I was a child. We talked and laughed. I got to cook for him again and hear stories of his life. It was hard to see the rock of our family in pain and hurting.

There was nothing we could do to fix it. He was a student of the bible and to see his faith waiver, shook me. I could not fight for him, but I could pray and support him through it as best I could. I watched him cry out to God in agony. My mom stood beside him crying. Someone wise once told me, to be to my parents what I had hoped they were to me. I took their advice. It has not been an easy walk but over the last 4 years, I have been very intentional to make sure I serve and honor them well. There were many days that I wanted to say, "Well they have not called me, so I will not call them." Then, I second guessed that thought and would pick the phone up anyway.

To add insult to injury, when I would talk to my siblings, it seemed like they talked to my dad all the time. I guess I assumed that he called them first. I never asked. At the end of the day, it mattered not who initiated their conversations. I still needed to do my part. I finally had a conversation with my siblings. It turned out my parents do not call them either. Funny how the enemy would whisper lies to me to cause division in our family. It did not win that time.

Dad had just finished his last chemo treatment. I witnessed his faith be restored. His relationship with God became deeper when I was diagnosed with COVID-19.

He took God at his word. He began to pray and build himself up in his most holy faith, by praying in the Holy Ghost. We had conversations about the Holy Spirit and though he taught the Word of God all the time, he admitted that he had not prayed in his heavenly language in quite some time. I believe that also provided a breakthrough in his healing. It forced him to put his complete faith and confidence in God.

In 2021, my dad was placed in hospice in March, and he passed away one month to the day that day on April 11, 2021. Earlier in the week, I had gone on spring break with my children to see my daughter in Atlanta.

We had a great week visiting the *Georgia Aquarium* and *Six Flags* theme park. We had my daughter's sisters with us. It was a really good time. Being away for that week allowed my siblings more time with mom and dad. On my return trip home, I sensed an urgency to get home. I wanted to go straight to dad but because we were in a pandemic my mom would not let me. I arrived home the day dad passed. He had my sister Facetime all his kids together, told us that he loved us, he was tired, and he was ready to go. He died before I could get from my house to theirs. That was the longest 34 minutes I ever experienced. He fought a good fight as a good soldier in Christ. The process of his transitioning was such a blessing. A year prior in 2020, he and mom had gotten their affairs in order, made me the executor of their estate, and made known their final wishes. All dad wanted was for all his family to come together once monthly and that none of his children or grandchildren left the earth before him. God and his children honored his wish. Though dad was sick and could not enjoy most activities we did; we were together, and we got to see him smile in the midst of all that he was going through. When mom and dad brought us together to discuss their affairs, dad shared his heart in a way I had never seen before.

He apologized for not being there, not knowing, not fathering us. He had gained so much knowledge and wisdom in his 71 years. He had a birthday in March and left us in April. He left us full of love and affection. I can say I know my daddy loved me. God allowed me to have complete restoration with my father before he passed. Even comical moments like when he was telling me his favorite book of the Bible "John" and his favorite Bible verse John 11:28. I asked him if I could preach his eulogy and my sister said, "No Daddy, don't let her do it."

I was somewhat of the *wild child* of the family. Dad laughed, rolled over, and acted like he was asleep.

We laughed so hard. He had so much joy even though he was in so much pain. Writing this brings tears to my eyes because I was just really getting to know my dad when he left this earth. His last two years were my best two years with him.

MESSAGE TO DADS:

Whether you want your child or not, they are here now. You shape who they are and how they interact with the world. Show them love and affection. Spend time with them, talk to them, and nurture them. For some of you, this may be hard because no one ever did that for you. Ask God to help you, He will. Read the Bible, read a book, pray, talk to another dad that you see doing the work, get counseling, and join a support group. You are needed. I do not care how mom makes it look like they have it all together, your child needs you too. If you are a co-parent, make the best of the situation. Keep the child first. Everything will not be "your" way. Be willing to compromise and keep your children safe. You are the protector! Protect your children by showering them with love and affection. Financial support is needed but your presence is most important.

IF PEOPLE PLEASER WAS A PERSON

We spent time with my mom's side of the family but not a lot of time with my dad's side. Mom would not let me go anywhere. I had to ask to go across the street. Whenever she was not home, I used to sneak out to see my friends or cousins or I would sneak people in after I put my sisters and brothers down for a nap. I knew when my parents would get home so I knew my exact window of opportunity. I had tons of responsibility and authority placed on me at such a young age.

Thinking back, I had more freedom and responsibility than I should have. At the time, I did not understand it. While I excelled in caring for my siblings, I failed at taking care of me.

All I ever wanted to do was make my mom happy. She was a stickler. She was very critical and judgmental towards me. To me, she seemed more concerned about what people thought and not how I felt. To her, my feelings seemed insignificant and non-existent. She was hard. What my mom said went, PERIODT! I heard the word "no" so much from her that I stopped asking for anything that I may have wanted.

Instead of asking her, I figured things out on my own. She was a stickler for time. If mom said to be ready to go by 9 am, that is exactly what she meant. By the time it was 9:01 or 9:15, she was long gone! After a few times chasing after the car after she left home, I got the message loud and clear: she was gone and not turning back! If my siblings and I were ready at the proper time, but our clothes failed to meet her standards, she left us home. If our chores or homework were not done, we were left at home. Though mom loved sports, loved her kids and loved all those she encountered; she played no games!

I learned that the critical spirit she carried was because of the way she was treated by her parents. While her parents were present for their other children, they did not seem to love her the same. Because of this, mom spent much of her time at her grandmother's home in a different county away from her siblings. I can imagine that she felt like she was not enough and because of this, she felt the need to be perfect in every way that she could control. She kept her house clean; she kept us kids clean and learned not to rely on others.

While this worked well for her, it was very difficult growing up in that type of atmosphere.

All I knew was that nothing I could do was right. If I cleaned the kitchen, she would say that the dishes were dirty and make me wash all of them again or pull all the dishes out of the cabinet and then I had to wash, dry and put them all away. I could clean the bathroom and then she would find something wrong with it and I would have to do it all over again. This carried over into my child-rearing. I did not have the autonomy to raise my son. I tried to teach him educational skills early and have him not drink sodas, eat junk, etc... and my parents would butt in and say, "Oh, let that boy have that," or they would just give him whatever I instructed him not to have.

Even outside the home with sports, mom would have a critique for everything. After completing a game, she would say to me, "You should have run faster, taken the shot, not taken the shot, why did you foul out?" Her critique of me was constant!

All the nonstop attacks combined with the molestation caused me to lose who I was. I lost my confidence. My self-esteem was shot. I did not feel loved. I did not have any self-worth. I did not love myself. I know many around me were likely thinking, "Anissa, you are not unattractive, what do you mean you didn't love yourself?"

Yet, no matter how pretty I was, how smart and responsible I was, self-love was not something I possessed. I allowed so many things to transpire in my life because of this. I would spend over 40 years of my life in this state. I put everyone else's well-being over my own. If someone around me needed anything I took care of them, even when it meant not meeting my own needs. I was a people pleaser to the core. I did what I thought people around me wanted because I did not have a voice. I could not please my mother, so I tried to please people, everyone else. I tried to please my family, my friends, my men, and my employer.

I spent so much time trying to please other people that I was very unhappy. I lacked identity. This manifested with me having sex with anyone I date. I became whatever the person around me desired. I felt like my purpose was to please other people. I had no sense of why God made me. I had a difficult time articulating what I enjoyed, because I did not know. I was like a chameleon. Whatever the people around me wanted, I wanted too. When people changed, my likes and desires changed too. I had a fear of disappointing people. It gripped me so tightly I could not grow as a person. I was stunted and felt stuck. My life felt useless.

CHAPTER 2
The Brokenness

INCEST

How could you sleep with your cousin? I thought you would never do that, said my aunt. Of course, I never planned on that happening, but it did. I thought my son was my then fiancé's child. There was no doubt in my mind until on my son's first birthday, my grandmother and aunt were discussing how my son looked like my great uncle so and so (my cousin that I had slept with looks like this uncle). Oops! Was my fiancé really not the father? I believed he was, and if he wasn't it was not a secret I would keep. I called my cousin whom I had secretly had a rendezvous with. I asked once again (as I had before) when we had sex, did you come? I also had to call the other potential fathers (there were 2 more guys) to ask the same question. You are probably wondering how I could not know who the father was. Well, over the years I had learned to dissociate. I could be somewhere and not be there all at the same time. I remembered who I had sex with and when, but I could not tell you what transpired, details were forgotten. I chose the one I thought was guilty because I awoke from my sleep with the evidence of ejaculation all over my legs. Initially, when I found out I was pregnant the two less likely guys (so I thought) had denied it.

You may ask, how could I sleep with my cousin? It was easy for me because this was something that my family had been doing for years. It was passed down to me through what psychologists called a generational cycle. I called it a generational curse. I fell victim to it. My parents fell victim to it.

One of my children's fathers fell victim to it. I knew this curse had to be broken but it first had to be exposed.

Why are all your kin folk so fine? I would not find out the real answers to these questions until I was an adult. When I was 47 years old, I uncovered many details regarding my family history. A family member exposed many intimate details of my family that had been hidden. As I consider this, maybe they were not hidden. Perhaps I had buried them under all the pain.

When I went around my family as a teenager, and even when I was slightly younger, I worried about how they sexualized my presence.

Some of the men had restraint, but most did not. There were instances where they would have me sit on their laps and force me to give them a kiss. It was during those times that I experienced the touches, the fondles, the gropes, and the lustful stares. It was with my family that my lustful appetite began. It was with my family that I first experienced being objectified sexually. I quickly learned to objectify other people as well. I did not view people as people or relationships as relationships, all I saw was warm bodies to fulfill my need. When I met new people, I automatically saw them as the next person to scratch the itch I had for more sex.

It did not matter who you were or if you were not available. If I wanted it, I had it. Because of this, I was often called a bitch, whore, slut, and whatever else you can think of, by those around me. Sadly, I referred to myself in those derogatory terms as well. It was sad.

Back to this incest thing, it was going on before me and my parents. A family member would get pregnant by another family member and the pregnant one would get shipped off to another family member and they would raise the child as their own. That sounds crazy right? It is crazy! What is worse is the family knew but everyone was under a secret gag order.

What goes on in this house stays in this house! That was the threat, the gag order. We were commanded to not say anything, ask anything, to not see anything or to forget anything that you witnessed happened.

My house, my home, my job, my family, my situation, it all overwhelmed me. I was pregnant with baby number four, and I was still a single woman. No hope of a future with my cousin, at least not for me. He had finally convinced his other cousin to marry him after years of dating. Although I had his child, I knew marriage, or a relationship would be worse. Once the DNA results came in, he swore me to secrecy from his soon-to-be wife. She married him and did not find out about us until years later when child support became an issue. He still lied to her, and she threatened me. Yet, I did not care about any of that, I only cared about the welfare of our son. This man refused to see our son or participate in any way because his wife threatened to leave him with their two daughters and take the house (that he built). He made his choice, so we all lived with it. His family was not involved with our son. I used to put forth the effort so he could know them, make calls, and send cards. Now, the relationship is relegated to major holidays and his birthday. His grandma used to try to make sure to send him something. Most times though they act like he does not exist. At first it was difficult, but we survived.

How did this whole incest thing get started? Someone in our family bloodline opened the door to this sin/behavior long before I was ever born but it was still very active in my family. Someone had to take a stand and stop it. That person would be me.

LONELINESS AND DEPRESSION

On the way home from a counseling session, it was raining and this song I had never heard before was playing on the radio. It was by Jason Nelson called

"Residue". The words that touched my heart and sent me to tears were:

> *When I'm with you*
> *I've got a new set of rules*
> *I can see the old me is through*
> *You leave no residue (no residue)*
> *'Cause you wash away*
> *Wash away, you wash away*
> *Wash away, yeah*
> *You make me new*
> *You leave no residue*

I knew that I was reaching the place where God was healing and changing me. I had to search my mind to find where the depression first started. The time I can remember is the year 1994. I was 24, the mom of three kids under ten. I was an E-3 in the Navy. I did not make a lot of money as daycare took most of it. My oldest son lived with me and his sisters. I was functionally depressed and overcome by loneliness. I did not fit in with the world anymore, but I also was not accepted by the church. I went to work and performed the tasks of my job well but once I arrived home, I escaped into a dark shell. I went to church, worshiped, and received teaching yet, I did not fit in because I was a young unmarried woman and had more kids than most people my age. A lot of the young church ladies were childless. Some of the people there would say they were there for me but whenever I needed them, they disappointed me.

There was always a lame excuse about their lack of support. For example, they would say, "Sis, if you need me to watch the kids for you, let me know." I would call the sister to make good on her promise, but I would receive endless excuses as to why she needed to renege on her promise. Either way, I still had to work. I was forced to find other options, sometimes down to the very last minute.

Men, well there was always one available whenever I needed them. If I wanted comfort or companionship, I had it. When I needed something from the store, they would always come through for me. If I wanted conversation, I could get that too. No matter what the favor was, it was always connected to sex. When these scenarios did not play out, I would watch television for hours on end. Many times, I would just stare at the screen as a measure of escape.

As a new Christian, I had just rededicated my life to Christ, so I was very conflicted within myself. My demons wanted to keep living but because of my convictions, I wanted them to die. I wanted them to go away. They would not seem to budge. I tried to get rid of them, but they seem to come back even stronger.

I needed help so I turned to the church, but they could not help me. The people from the church just admonished me to pray, and read my bible, to renew my mind. None of that made sense to me. I tried to do those things but at night when my urges were the strongest my demons would come back with a greater intensity than before. My dreams, my imagination, and my conversations all were filled with sex.

Even in church, during worship, I would have flashbacks of very vivid scenes of a sexual encounter.

I did not have a lot of female friends, so most of the people I talked to extensively were males. Most of them had ulterior motives even if they seemed friendly at first. These conversations happened all day every day. I tried my best to control these thoughts and conversations more during the day, yet, this battle of good and evil that was going on inside of me took its toll.

I was so tired of hearing men use this scripture reference about how the spirit is willing, but the flesh is weak. This scripture is taken out of context to justify sin. In that very same scripture, it says to watch and pray so you do not enter into temptation. Many seemed to enjoy making a mockery of God and my beliefs. I felt so alone. I wondered often about who I could talk to with and share what was going on inside of my head and within my body?

Who would listen, be able to help, and not judge me or beat me over the head with the Bible?

Most of the women I tried to talk to about what was happening in my life were so judgmental. Everything I hoped they would not do, they did instead. They would say, "Girl, if you love God then you would not sin. Why can't you be like me, I haven't slept with a man in 10 years, 20 years, etc." My hope was to get through a month or two without having sex. Sometimes my goal was just to try to make it through the day without sex. Though I could quote tons of scriptures I still struggled in the area of my sexuality. I knew the scriptures, but it felt impossible to live them out. During these times of struggle, I would retreat to watching mindless hours of TV, skip doing chores, and I would allow the rest of my life to spiral out of control. I would talk on the phone for hours about nothing or plot with my next hook-up situationship. My self-worth was in the toilet and my self-love was on zero. Yet and still, I wanted love, attention, and affection. The devil never failed to deliver. Sex was my tool of choice in overcoming loneliness and depression. A warm body next to me provided temporary relief to whatever I was feeling overwhelmed with at the time.

Whether it was because I felt rejected because my kid's father did not pick me or want to be with me or even in the life of our child. I was overwhelmed. I had so many responsibilities from a very young age, and I was expected to just handle it. But I handled it with sex. Ultimately, making all these illegitimate connections and causing even more problems in my life. In addition to being alone and depressed, I added more guilt and shame. While my goal was not to sleep with this man or that man it seemed to come with the territory of me finding comfort. I got to the point where I hated myself so much that I wished I were fat and ugly hoping that men would no longer find me attractive. I almost ate myself to that place but thank God for good genes and His grace in preventing me from going too far overboard. I began having headaches, problems with my bowels, and reflux. I did go to the doctor for the pain I experienced, but they were only able to treat the symptoms. The mental and emotional distress I was experiencing began to manifest in my body. My stress level was high. I quickly learned that I could not fight spiritual wars using natural methods. While I knew I still needed to manage the natural symptoms, I knew I would need to do the intense work to become whole.

Loneliness plagued me for many years. For me, loneliness resembled being at work with an entire crew yet, being disconnected from everyone. Most of my co-worker were party goers, or our interests did not match. Loneliness was me attending a megachurch where I would come every week, see regular parents who also had children in daycare, yet we never formed any authentic relationships outside of church. Or, it looked like having a house full of kids, but no one to support you. I often experienced a deep longing that never faded away. Sometimes this feeling felt more pronounced than others. When the feeling became too overwhelming, I would fill the void with sexual relationships. I would meet a guy and not pay attention to the red flags. Many times, we lacked common interest, and I would not even be physically attracted to him, but agreed because he was physically and sexually available for me. This happened consistently. It was a perpetual cycle that went on and on for years. It was the same scenario, with a different dude. It was like I was a revolving door with a NEXT sign plastered on my face.

I dated this other guy out of pure loneliness. He was not the most attractive, yet I knew he liked me, so I used it to my advantage. We worked together indirectly. I worked in radiology; he worked in the supply department. I had a solid professional working relationship with him. We exchanged numbers outside of work and began dating. He lived minutes away from my house, so it was quite convenient for us to hook up. At times he would come to my house after the kids were in bed. We claimed we would "watch movies" at least that is what I told him. He believed me. In actuality, he was just being used to feed my habit.

I would go on and on for years in this manner. It was not until I went to counseling that I realized the impact this had on my life. I was empty, void of love and of inner peace.

The relationships I engaged in never involved emotional ties. The men did not care about me. At times this made me sad, then angry. I was mostly angry at myself. I was angry at my desperation and my acceptance of the bare minimum from them in exchange for their time. I was in a horrible place.

MORE RECENTLY: 2021

I began seeing a counselor. My counselor is a pastoral counselor. She has been formally trained as well as trained by the Holy Spirit. Our work in therapy is centered on me tearing down the lies that I have believed about myself. It is one thing to take on what people put on you, but it is a whole different creature to believe the lies you tell yourself. The lies and limiting beliefs that I had were so deeply ingrained. When I completed my self-esteem assessment I lied as a measure of self-protection. While lying was not my intention, it helped me continue my cover. I would not allow anyone to see the real me. They could only see what I wanted them to see. Why would I lie to my counselor? She is trying to help me. When I realized what happened, immediately after my session, I began to weep and journal. What happened to make me feel that way? Whose voice was I listening to? God, Holy Spirit, my parents, friends, exes, or all of the above? Talking to God through journaling helped me to get to the root. I addressed what I was feeling and why I was feeling it. I shared it with my counselor in my next session and it was so beneficial to my process. Though I am no longer controlled by my past behaviors, the lies were so deeply embedded that they still affected my daily life, relationships, and the way I showed up for myself.

LOW SELF-ESTEEM, LOW SELF-WORTH

Low self-esteem and low self-worth made me question and doubt everything. My intelligence, my confidence, my ability to fully show up as a parent, daughter, employee, leader, sister, friend, etc. I attached my value to what I did and not who I was. I did not realize they were not the same. I remember going through a counseling session some years ago. I was distraught because I had sex after not having sex for an extended period. I beat myself up as usual and my counselor stopped me. He said repeat after me, "I did what I did, but I am not what I did. I did what I did but I am not what I did." I stopped. He said, who told you to stop? Keep saying it. So, I continued, "I did what I did but I am not what I did. I did what I did but I am not what I did. I did what I did but I am not what I did."

My prayer for you is that even as you are reading this, as you repeat the phrase the spirit of God will set you free just as he did me in that moment. The act, your actions do not define who you are. You can change, I did.

TOLL ON MY MENTAL HEALTH

Remember a couple of chapters ago when I talked about growing up under a critical spirit? Child molestation and a critical spirit took a toll on my mental health. What comes easily for most may take me longer and be a more difficult task.

Church folk often over-spiritualize mental health issues. I was not allowed space to express my hurt or pain. Many times, they did not realize the additional hurt they were imposing on me by not permitting my voice to be heard.

I have an undiagnosed mental illness. Yet, I waited to receive treatment once I was outside the military. This treatment came through counseling. I have been under the care of a counselor on and off for years, secretly. My first encounter with a counselor was when my pastor realized that my sexual encounters were not just me being a young person, but it was an addiction. She set me up with a counselor. It was there I discovered my son's father was not who I thought he was and that I was molested as a child. A few years later, my son's psychotherapist spent time counseling me. I would take my son to his appointment. His counselor would recognize that I was not myself. He would send my son out to play while he and I talked. I had a friend who was a counselor, she received plenty of practice with me and I received plenty of free counseling. I have tried theophostic counseling with a beautiful couple in Springfield, Massachusetts. I did exercises to try to change the way I saw myself and how to prepare myself for a future healthy relationship. I counseled with one of the associate ministers in Cambridge, Massachusetts some years later. The elder was a physician's assistant.

My sessions helped me to grow spiritually yet I still found myself in sexual encounters though not nearly to the degree as in times past. In 2016, I received prophetic counseling. I was in counseling last year and as soon as I am assigned a new counselor, I will be in therapy again. Counseling has helped save my life.

As I write this, I realize that I have held this hurt and pain inside for decades. I have been an emotional wreck. I have hidden my pain and know that it is time to unveil it. It is time for me to heal as this pain has spilled into all aspects of my life. Fear is the real reason I do not date or go anywhere to meet people to date. Deep down, I feel like it is just something else for me to mess up or someone else to take advantage of me. I have given so much to men who used me for sex, and they would continue in this way if I had allowed it.

Anxiety and fear impacted me and my educational pursuits. It was paralyzing. Often, I would see the academic work and begin to count myself out before I even start the work. On top of this, it is difficult for me to maintain focus. My children often have difficulty in school and in their emotions. I've spent countless time questioning my ability and capacity to help them. I ask, "How could I help them when I have not even helped myself?"

Anxiety caused my neck and back to tighten up to the point where it is painful. It appears I carry all this garbage from my head in my gut. I am bloated frequently. I spend much of my day in the bathroom. If I am not emotionally eating because of anxiety, then I do not eat at all for fear of bloating and being uncomfortable all over again. I cannot fit any of my clothes. I do not want to buy new ones. I want to gain control of this part of my life. I am tired of the negative thoughts controlling the narrative of my life. Spiritually, I continue to tell myself, "You just need to fast to break this thing off of your life." Fasting is important, but I also need a counselor that will give me a safe place to just let it all out, no judgment. I had a psychological evaluation recently. It felt good to let some of my secrets out. Things that I have refused to share with everyone. I just want to get to the place where my self-talk is positive and healthy. I often second-guess myself wondering about the what-ifs of life. When I discussed this with my doctor, he prescribed medication for ADD to help me focus. I had just gone through a hormonal episode that threw me for a loop. I would have intense hot flashes that lit my body on fire and drenched me from head to toe. Immediately following, I would be freezing, sleeping and need tons of water. A side effect of the medication was drowsiness. This meant I could not operate a vehicle. Drowsiness was another drawback. In order to complete assignments for school, or to drive for a ride share company part-time, to supplement my income, I needed to ask the doctor for a different medication.

The doctor referred me to Veterans Affairs (VA) because he said they have more resources for me there. I called to begin the process to request a medication change and a psychological evaluation. I received my initial screening the next day. However, my medication appointment was not until three months later.

Thank goodness I had a decent relationship with Jesus. Other veterans were worse off and suicidal. I am grateful that was not my testimony, yet I still needed help.

What was I to do with the depression I suffered? There were many days of irrational beliefs and negative thoughts, oversleeping and overeating. The pandemic increased some of these feelings for me. I love people, touching them, hugging them, talking to them and the lack of human interaction deflated me. I cried seemingly for no reason. I needed to do deep soul work and I needed assistance in doing so. This type of work should not be done alone.

If you are finding yourself in the same place, here are some practical strategies to consider. Begin to celebrate the good things and people in your life. Celebrate small victories. The fact that you woke up this morning, bathed, and made your bed is an accomplishment. Of course you have tons more on your to-do lists. Remember that you always have tomorrow. Set realistic expectations and do not put unnecessary pressure on yourself. When you do not meet your original goals, it is okay. If you are too hard on yourself, you will continue the cycle of nothingness.

I have always had high functioning depression. Because of this, whenever I told someone about my depression, they barely believed me because I performed well. Failure was not an option for me. I was raised to be perfect. I soon discovered that no one could live the perfect lie. Lying only hurts you in the long run.

If you find yourself in this dark place of depression here are some practical tools to push through to improve your well-being:

- **Be yourself, flaws and all**: Embrace your authentic self, acknowledging that imperfections are part of what makes you unique and valuable.
- **Love yourself**: Practice self-compassion and acceptance, recognizing your worth and inherent value as a person.
- **Lose the negative self-talk:** Challenge and replace derogatory self-talk with affirming and uplifting words. Refrain from labeling yourself with negative terms such as "dumb," "stupid," or "crazy."
- **Replace negative words with positive ones**: Incorporate positive affirmations, preferably drawn from scriptures or other sources of inspiration, to counteract negative thoughts and beliefs.
- **Work out**: Engage in physical activity, even if it's as simple as taking a daily walk. Exercise has numerous physical and mental health benefits, and you'll likely feel a significant improvement in your overall well-being.

- **Seek therapy**. God designed us to work alongside someone else. Research caring counselors who are equipped to handle even your most difficult need.

CHAPTER 3
The Identity Struggle

AN ALL-OUT WAR

Amid a heated night of passion with a much older gentleman, he stopped as though scared. It was as if he had seen a ghost. He said he had only experienced this one other time in his life. He was almost 70 but looked 45, no lie! He began to preach to me. He asked why I was doing this. He began to tell me that the causal nature of our sexual encounter was not a reflection of who I truly was. He told me that I was worth more than that moment. He poured out so much that day. I knew right away that it was God speaking to me through him. It shook me to the point that I left and went home physically shaking. I was never the same.

Yet, at times I struggled in feeling like I was multiple people. You may be asking; how could one person have several different personalities? Trauma was the cause of this reality. I was introduced to pain early in my childhood. After a while, I created a way to escape whatever was my current reality.

This creates splits in the soul where characters and personas appear and become who I had to become to survive.

Anissa

Let's meet Anissa. Anissa was a professional businesswoman, she was very intelligent, and well-put-together. She operated in excellence and is very personable. Anissa is dedicated, loyal, and a hard worker. She follows the rules because that is what is expected of her. Anissa's younger version was a people pleaser. She tried to make everyone happy even if it meant she was miserable. You would most likely meet Anissa at work.

Buffy/Bomquisha

Buffy was a bad girl. She was every bit of an alpha female and could have her way with just about anyone. Occasionally she would meet her match but for the most part she controlled things and people. She especially controlled men. If Buffy wanted it, she had it. Buffy was fully controlled by her flesh and feelings of lust. It did not matter if you belonged to someone else, if Buffy wanted you, it was a wrap. Buffy talked a lot of junk but backed it up. When Buffy got really out of hand, Bomquisha showed up and out. Bomquisha was a more ratchet version of Buffy if there could be such a thing. Bomquisha seemed to have a radar for her next unsuspecting victim. It was like a magnet to draw men who were ready and willing. No words needed to be spoken, it was a look. She looked at you, and you looked at her and you both knew what time it was.

Evangelist

You could meet Evangelist at church at work or anywhere. Evangelist was so deeply ingrained in Anissa that even when Anissa tried to turn her off, it did not work. People with any discernment knew that she did not belong in the environments, relationships, or conversations she tried to force her way into. Evangelist would meet nice people and Buffy and Bomquisha would interfere. Those two would turn an innocent encounter into something it was never intended to be. Evangelist was just trying to witness and share her love for Christ and then conversations and activities were hijacked by those two. They operated in tandem. Buffy would bait you and Bomquisha came in for the kill.

Sunshine

Let's just say that Sunshine was the icing on the cake. Very few have ever gotten to experience Sunshine. It took a special person to get to this level. If they arrived at this level, the person was more than likely her equal. This person would have multiple personalities as well just as bad as hers.

Sunshine and her partner would recognize it in each other. This made for an experience that seemed to be quite out of this world. Sunshine and these partners enjoyed every part of each other, EVERY PART! They connected, emotionally, naturally, physically, and spiritually. Even those who did not practice their faith regularly were affected. Sunshine was so enjoyable; her partner could not handle it. Sunshine's partners could not handle the level of emotions that came from their union. As much as they enjoyed Sunshine's company and all they received, it was too overwhelming, a too good-to-be-true feeling or I'm going to go crazy if I keep messing with you. There have been instances where after meeting someone and just having a few conversations, they recognized Sunshine and almost immediately took a pass. They had a family member who had schooled them, or they had an experience with someone similar. I was something else.

HELP I DON'T WANT TO BE A HOE NO MO!

You weren't a hoe, were you? Yes, I was! Did I want to be? NO. What I did was who I thought I was. I thought sex was all I was good for. Let me define what a hoe is. A person who sleeps around only interested in sex or money. The bible or church folks would call it being a whoremonger. People in the streets call it what it was, a hoe, a tramp, a slut, just *loose*, and probably many more names that I have not mentioned.

My flesh craved other bodies. If I wanted sex, I had it. At the time, I did not know that a woman's body naturally experienced cycles. I felt my flesh was leading me around like a dog in heat. Of course, there was always someone available to quench my thirst. This was so out of hand. I had *play dates* while my kids were in school, and I worked at night. Marital status did not matter, if I wanted you and you wanted me, it was on. This had become dangerous, because I could not stop. I did not think I could ever live without sex. Masturbation was not my thing. In my mind, there were no substitutes, I was strictly dickly!

No one knew the intensity of the life I lived. I could not talk to anyone about what I was experiencing because of the fear of judgment from church folks. The "you know better speeches" I did not want to hear. Nor did I want to be beat over the head with scriptures. I needed answers and I needed them fast. I wanted to be free from this way of life. Constantly giving myself to people and spending time with people who did not care about me, was a drag. Most people only wanted what we could do for each other. It has been coined "warm body syndrome". It did not matter who it was, I just needed a body. I cannot believe some of the people I hooked up with now. In my freshman year of college, my bestie and I sat down and wrote on a sheet of lined college-ruled notebook paper the number of partners we had. I filled up both sides, two per line. Let me help you, there were 25 lines multiplied by 2 equals 50 people. I was only 18. I may have only been 17 if it was before our birthdays. When people say it is a small world, believe them. Be careful of the name you make for yourself!

I methodically planned who I would mess around with in various parts of town. They still knew each other and talked.

I had one in the northside, east end, west end, southside, and folks from out of town, military men. I equated sex with power. I had the power, so I thought. Really, I was being controlled by Satan. I thought like a man, not a woman. They thought they were getting over on me when it was I who played the game well. I had one man going out the back door while one was coming in the front. One man in the morning, one for lunch, and another for dinner. This followed me into the Navy, some guy would call ahead to my next duty station (job) and give a rundown of me to their homeboys. They would say, "Man, you heard about Jones? Yeah, man, all you have to do is act like you're a Christian, go to church with her, or tell her you want her to be your wife or something like that, and man, you can get that thang." I was cold and numb to any of the insults or the fact that there was no love involved.

Finally, it got old, real old. I remember a situationship that did not quite go the way I intended. After a hookup, I realized that this was no longer cost-effective. I drove 45 minutes to meet a guy to cook for him (an expensive, exotic dish) and get my sexual fix. He did not pay me back for the ingredients or my gas. That encounter wasted my time, and it cost me my money. I wish I could say it stopped there, but it did not. I could not go to anyone in my church at the time, my friends and family had no idea how bad it was (if they knew it was because they had similar tendencies). What was I to do? Just like games recognize game, spirits recognize spirits! I sought hard after God. Matthew 17:21 says that some things only come out by prayer and fasting was no longer just a spiritual reference but was something my life depended on it.

I was at my breaking point, a place of complete surrender to God.

God, what do I need to do? I had to deny myself and pick up my cross. I had to deny myself sex and stay away from anyone to whom I had a strong attraction. I fasted, prayed, and memorized scriptures. These are scriptures that I had to remind myself of constantly. Here are some I remember right off top: John 15:7-If I abide in him and he abides in me I can ask what I will, and it shall be done unto me. Hebrews 12:1-Lay aside every weight and the sin that so easily besets you. Galatians 5:7-You did run well, who did hinder you? Galatians 6:7-8/2 Tim 2:22-Whatsoever a man sows that he shall also reap, if you reap to your spirit, life everlasting, if you reap to your flesh, eternal damnation, flee youthful lust, and lastly, Romans 12:1 present your body as a Holy sacrifice unto God. Holy Spirit was teaching me all that I needed to know.

This was the beginning stage of my deliverance. I began to pray the word of God over myself. The word protected me from me. God's word was a shield. Some of the hook-ups I would try to make just would not work on my end, on their end, scheduling conflicts, etc. God blocked it! With each victory, I gained more strength. This was God taking me from glory to glory!

In 1996, God began to soften my heart. I remember it so clearly. I was sitting in the rear of the church (it was a large church) on the right. I normally sat in the back on the left by the children's church so if my number was called for my child, I would have an easy exit. The pastor was preaching on 1

Thessalonians 4:4, that each of you knows how to control your own body in holiness (sanctification) and honor. He talked about wolves in sheep's clothing, and men and women in the house of God. How some come just to look for prey, and so forth. He said to ask God to show you what is hindering you from living holy. I prayed that prayer on a Thursday and by that Tuesday my pastor's wife was calling me in the office. I did not mention that I sang in the choir and on that Sunday, I had a big ole hickey on my neck that I did not notice, but she did. This is where I began counseling for my addiction. This was not by chance. I was a member of a very large ministry. I normally sat on the left side of the church, near the children's church, just in case my kids' number was called. This particular night, I was on the right side, right in front of my pastor's office. I never sat there. As my pastor's wife passed by me, she tapped me to come with her. We sat in her office, and she asked me how many people I had been with (it was only around February). The answer was, I had already slept with 7 people. She then said she thinks it is more than a matter of me just being young, but this is a problem. I tried to tell her the first time we talked. I knew it was a problem. She sent me to counsel with a counselor that worked for the church. I enjoyed these sessions because someone was interested in me, the real me. Not the professional me that people saw at work but the me that had been hurting for a very, long time. I was able to be open and honest. This is when I revealed that I had an abortion, that I did not know who the father of my son was and where I found out I had been molested as a child.

      Until I met with my counselor, I did not remember my childhood from about age 6-8, I could only remember walking into the room with my cousins. One of my cousins said come here and suck my dick. I remember him taking me outside and forcing me to get down on my knees and do just that. It was at that point that I learned to be somewhere and act like I was not there. I could perform sexual acts and not remember what transpired. I could remember who and where but not what happened. This threw men that I had sex with off. I was very cold. I mean ice, cold. I could be intimate with you and still ignore you like a stranger. It made me very insensitive. This went on for years until I accepted Jesus as my Lord and Savior as a young adult. I wish I could say I was instantly delivered and set free from all of my immoral ways. It was still a long journey. I was learning more about Christ, but I did not know how to live without sex. I liked sex more than food. When I craved it, I craved it. It was an appetite that could not be extinguished. My counseling was going well until she left then I was left. I had one real friend that I could talk to. He was a white guy that was older than me and a virgin. He was not trying to get anything from me. He genuinely cared for me as a person. I loved the time we spent together just talking and hanging out. It meant so much to me because he was not trying to get into my panties. This friendship was halted abruptly because my pastor intervened and told him to stop spending time with me because I was pregnant with another man's baby. I was forced to deal with the guy I 'thought' the baby was by. I secretly resented him. He did not understand me, and he was always kissing and fondling me instead of waiting like other Christian couples, or so I thought. He was very jealous. I did not cheat on him, but he made me wish I had. One time I was on the phone with my male friend, and I did not answer the other line. This man showed up at my door trying to get into my house. I had asked him to do something for me and he said no. Of course, I had someone else to do it. He was jealous that someone else helped me, I did not care. When he just popped up unannounced, he got his feelings hurt because I did not open the door. My platonic friend could hear everything. It was really bad. He was accusing me of having someone else in my house. Losing my engagement ring was the best thing that happened to me (I think my son gave it to one of his girlfriends). I was grateful for my then-fiancé's assistance during a time in my life when my children were too much for me to handle alone. He helped to raise them. He was a good father figure, but he was not right for me. Then I started counseling with a woman that I loved going to see but like the church counselor she suddenly moved away. My counseling stopped, I could not go into my job at the Navy and say hey, "I'm a sex addict I need help."

I had a friend who was a counselor, and our talks were very therapeutic. One of my male children began to act out at home and school to the point I took him to counseling. His counselor was amazing. He interviewed us and began my son's therapy. In some sessions he did not see my son but counseled me instead. He could see that I was physically present but not mentally whole. This is where I was initially unofficially diagnosed with multiple personality disorder. The only person I could tell was my friend who was also a counselor. I felt it was not safe for me to have people thinking I was crazy. But this was pride. If you are in this state, do not let this stop you from getting the help you need.

Even still I was a people pleaser so I could not have that revealed, it must remain a secret. My son and I had sessions with him until my son's visits expired. I was in a good church that gave me a good bible foundation. I grew quickly in my relationship with God and He made me whole in my mind.

However, I never felt like I was good enough. No matter what I did or how I did it. It was not good enough. "Do that again" kept ringing in my ears. Because my mom was a real stickler and wanted things "her way!" it created a "people-pleasing" monster in me. I would do almost anything for anybody, even if I did not feel like it or did not have time for it. That critical spirit followed me everywhere. It was the "monkey on my back", I could not shake it. Even at work, I felt I needed to be better than the next person. If I did not do it better, I felt inferior, like I was not good enough. I did not know that my role was not my identity. This played into why it was so hard for me to surrender my body to God. Not only did I enjoy sex, but it was one of the few things I thought I was pretty good at. There were always plenty of men to remind me of that. However, I got to the place where I was tired of all conversations being sexual. Even if they did not start there, they finished there. My imagination was vivid, full-color flashbacks of my sexual encounters. How could I break free from these constant flashbacks and memories? *I tried time and time again only to fail and give in just one more time. That one time would turn into a season of failure. A cycle that seemed unbreakable.* One month, 4 months, 7 months, 9 months then that one person would catch my eye, open my heart with lies and there I go again. I used to say, "I just want to live without sex for one year. Just one year, please. I got to the point where the moon and my body ruled me. If there was a full moon, I wanted sex. I just wanted sex all the time, moon or not! I knew it was unhealthy and unnatural, but I could not seem to stop.

I did not have many relationships, but had many "sexships", "hookups" "booty calls", whatever you want to call them. They are commonly referred to now as "situationships". I was sick of my body, my flesh, ruling me in that way. I finally decided that enough was enough and declared to God that I needed His help. I needed true deliverance at all costs. I no longer wanted to trade addictions, sex for alcohol, alcohol for food, or sex for depression. I wanted out, Lord, please help me!

The journey out was not as hard as I thought it would be. I had believed the devils, people, and the lies I had been telling myself for so long. These lies became my truth: "No one will ever want you with all those kids, you're a freak, you must have some good (stuff), you are used goods, and you will be single forever."

As I began my journey, the lie became: "Your standards are too high, we all sin and fall short of God's glory. God knows your heart." This was only to break down any boundaries I was trying to set. One of the biggest wounds I suffered was when my dad said, "If a man is helping you to take care of you and your kids, then he expects to have sex with you." As if that was a guaranteed entitlement to someone I was not married to. He was referring to my fiancée at the time but still, we were not married. My dad was the epitome of being a Christian. You know you open the dictionary, and his picture would be beside the definition. When he implied that I should be having sex with my fiancée for all the "things" he was doing for me, I was shocked and deeply wounded. At that moment I felt all the lies I heard over the years were justified. It must be true. I felt like I was just a piece of tail. To hear from my dad was devastating. He was supposed to cover me, protect me, love me, and guide me. It was clear whose side he was on, clearly NOT MINE! This created an additional father wound for me. It would be many years before I brought someone home again. I had to make sure everything was perfect. By that I mean, we are engaged, not having sex, he believed in God too and he can speak intelligibly without embarrassing me. He had to be perfect. That was exhausting. I'm so glad that is over.

A TIME TO RECONCILE

To heal, I had to become self-aware and become one with God and myself. I had to be honest and do the work. It took staying in God's word, praying, fasting, and rehearsing the good things God says about me, his daughter. God reconciles us (brings us back together to himself). He has made us ministers of reconciliation according to his teachings in 1 Corinthians 5:17-19.

In the next chapter, we will explore this journey of healing in more detail.

CHAPTER 4
The Liberation

MY FREEDOM

My freedom only took 35 years. Yes, you read that right. 35. That is a long time. Why did it take so long? I liked my sin. I thought it was who I was. My alter ego ran my life. I had no clue who Anissa was. I knew who I wanted her to be but could not make the connection. I tried and tried but Buffy kept resisting and rising. Anissa had to take over or she was going to die. I was headed to dying a spiritual and literal death.

Buffy was going to kill Anissa! How was Buffy going to do that? Buffy's sex partners were dangerous! Most were married or in relationships where they lied about their status. I'll give you an example. I was in love with Great! That's the real nickname we used for him; he was concerned about his digital footprint. We met on my deployment. We spent a lot of time together. We got to know each other during the time we were there. It probably did not help that he was very handsome and thought his wife was cheating on him too. We both were very vulnerable. This deployment was only the second time I had been away from my children for an extended period in my life. He understood me. He took the time to listen. He loved children and wanted more, a son. I had a son he could love and adore. I could have more children and his wife could not. I considered moving to his city and being his second family when I retired. I loved him that much. It sounds crazy now, but at the time he was meeting a need that no one had ever met before. The wake-up call was when we got back to the US. He came to a city near me for training, so we saw each other. It was like no time had passed when I saw him. I was supposed to see him again while he was in town. My trip was suddenly halted. I believe his wife was tracking him or he was using me to regain her attention from her boyfriend. Whatever the case, I knew that she was suddenly coming to town and that he had bought a new gun for her for Christmas. I was happy to take a pass. I was WOKE at that moment and over the thought of moving. I did value my life. This is the same man who called me to tell me he was HIV positive. He was tested before going on another deployment. I was also tested, and my test was negative. He called back to let me know that his test was a false positive. I can take a hint.

    I also remember a time when it was late at night, and I was driving home from church. I passed by the turn for my house. I was tired of being stuck in this cycle. Free from sex for a while then back in the sheets with the next person. I will never forget this one day that changed my life. Buffy told Anissa to keep driving towards the oceanfront to take her life by running off the road. It was as if I was in a daze for a moment. She said she would kill me. I immediately came to myself, turned around, and went back home.

Then there was the time I received a phone call from a former sexual partner who said his HIV test came back positive and the only people he had slept with were me and his wife. I was still active-duty military, so I received HIV testing annually but I was tested after he called and followed up 6 months later to make sure. My results were negative, and he said he had a false positive. At least that was what he told me. I only cared that mine was negative.

On another occasion, I was stationed with this guy for a second time. We had messed around years before. He was one of the potential fathers of one of my older kids. He was the one caught up. He was young. He was very secretive. I honestly had forgotten he was married. He was just collecting the check from having a dependent wife. He was not sending her any money. I became pregnant with his child and miscarried. This time I was the one with feelings. We worked together so when I had some complications with the miscarriage, I asked him to take me to the hospital. No one knew we were seeing each other (only his best friend). He looked me right in the face and said no he could not leave. I do not know which was more painful that day. The physical pain I was in that had me bent over, or the pain of his rejection. He could have taken me to the doctor but chose not to that day. Shortly thereafter, I had a warning dream with dark figures that moved very quickly running around my home. They set my home on fire. It was like some type of storm hit my home. Furniture was thrown all over the house like a hurricane had hit my house, one of my children was missing and there was a hole in the wall. I immediately woke up from this dream with a sense of urgency. It felt real. I was breathing rapidly. I ran upstairs to check on my children. They were all present and accounted for. The dream showed me that this dude was involved in some dark stuff and if I continued to deal with him there would be some grave consequences. I could not afford it. I stopped seeing him and never looked back.

I needed God in a real way. Scripture saved my life. Romans chapter 8 is a passage of life in the spirit and the assurance of hope. It was a chapter that I felt led by the Holy Spirit to memorize in its entirety. My life has been reflective of my disobedience to not only memorize but adhere to the teachings in this chapter. As a survivor of child sexual assault, God was trying to communicate His love for me as a father, but I did not want to nor could I receive it. I thought he was punishing me. As I refer to it now, it brings hope and healing. God's love for us is not performance-based. I now realize why it was such a challenge for me to memorize this chapter in the Bible. 1996 was a monumental year. God told me to memorize Romans chapter 8. This chapter had so many answers for my life, there were many revelations. Firstly, God does not condemn me, He loves me as a Father. Secondly, that He prays for me and wanted the best for me. Third, the whole world is waiting on me to be "me". Fourth, the Holy Spirit convicts you of sin. He brings it to your attention. He does not beat you up about your sin or keep reminding you of it. Fifth, if you confess your sins, Jesus is faithful and just to forgive you your sins and cleanse you from all unrighteousness. Lastly, "NOTHING" can separate me from him. I'm no longer a slave!!!

To prove His love for us, the first thing he says in Romans 8:1-2, "There is therefore now no condemnation to them which are in Christ Jesus, who walk not after the flesh, but after the Spirit. For the law of the Spirit of life in Christ Jesus hath made me free from the law of sin and death (World Publishing, 1989). He does not condemn us, He loves us. The Holy Spirit helps us to live a life pleasing to God. When the Spirit of God leads us, he calls us sons of God. He adopted us as his sons into his kingdom. We can call him Abba (Father). He then speaks of how others are waiting for us to present Jesus to them and even we have the same expectation to show up. The words groaning and travailing remind me of childbirth. It can be painful and hard but the reward of the birth of a child is priceless. The Spirit prays for us even when we do not know what to pray for. God is so protective of His children that He will not allow anything to separate us from His love. This is so powerful, and He reminded me of this recently. This became my prayer. "For I am persuaded, that neither death, nor life, nor angels, nor principalities, nor powers, nor things present, nor things to come, nor height, nor depth, nor any other creature, shall be able to separate us from the love of God, which is in Christ Jesus our Lord, v.38." (World Publishing, 1989).

CHAPTER 5
The Journey To Wholeness

MOVING FORWARD

The road to becoming whole has been a journey. I would say it started when I was 22. It has been a process that has involved Christian psychotherapy, counseling, theophostic counseling, prayer, memorizing scripture, fasting, deliverance, a good strong church family, friends that challenge me, accountability, love, and a God that loves me even if I stumble and fall. I never have to prove my love to Him. God's acceptance of me is not based on my performance. Some would say it does not take all that. I am here to tell you it takes all of that unless God miraculously delivers you and you receive inner healing. That can happen. It just did not happen to me like that. I used to wish it happened like that for me. I wished I could just be normal like I thought everyone else was. I did not realize everyone has a struggle, a test of some sort. Today, I appreciate the path my life has taken. God has used me to touch many lives and through my transparency in writing this book, I am assured that He will reach so many more. I have my voice back and will be the voice for those who cannot speak yet. I believed the lies too long that I was not good enough, that no one will ever want me because I had seven kids, I had too much baggage. I believed that I was not worthy of love and affection. I believed that my sin was too great and because of that I would be disqualified from becoming a wife.

I am grateful to God that none of the whispers from the enemy about me are true. God has forgotten about all those mistakes and has tossed my sins into the sea of forgetfulness, as far as the east is from the west. He does not remember them anymore, so I do not have to remember them either.

I am beautiful, I am loved, I am forgiven, I am healed, I am delivered, I am free. I am 53. I like this new chapter. I am no longer a people pleaser. I am okay with saying no. I can set boundaries and keep them. I am no longer a dumping ground for others. I face my fears and submit them immediately to God. I have a heavenly Father who loves me and a natural father and mother who sacrificed a lot just for me to be here. I am humbled and excited about the opportunity for God to use me to be a blessing to you. Even if this book just touches one person, they can get free from the lies. It was worth every tear, every loss, every lesson learned, and every victory. You can get past your past too!

Here is another scripture for keeping, Philippians 3:14 "Forgetting those things that are behind and pressing forward to the mark of the prize of the High calling of God in Christ Jesus." Let's make it normal to no longer keep secrets. ***What goes on in this house will not stay in this house any longer!*** What went on in your house is free to go and be released. There is no burden that is unbearable to God. Release it to Him and watch freedom and deliverance be your guide to a fulfilling and abundant life.

CALL TO SALVATION

If you have never accepted Jesus as your Lord and Savior, let us take this moment, as you invite Him into your heart. It really is as simple as *ABC*. Repeat this prayer out loud:

A. "God, I come before you, **acknowledging** that I am a sinner."
B. "I **believe** in my heart that Jesus is your Son, that He died on the cross for my sins, and that He rose again on the third day."
C. "I **confess** with my mouth and believe in my heart that you have saved me. In Jesus' name, I pray. Amen!"

Welcome to your new life in Christ! As you embark on this journey, I encourage you to connect with a bible-believing church and engage with your new family in Christ. Begin feeding your spirit with the Word of God, just as you nourish your body with food. Consider starting your reading journey with the book of Acts or the gospel of John.

If this message has touched your heart, I encourage you to share it with someone else who may need to experience the freedom and love found in Christ. Remember, I'm cheering you on as you step into the victory that awaits you!

About the Author

Meet Anissa Jones – Life Coach, Consultant, and Career Counselor extraordinaire! Her mission? To see women thrive in every aspect of their lives, inside and out. Armed with a certification in Inner Healing and Deliverance, she's all about helping women uncover their purpose and map out the road to success.

But that's not all – Anissa's also the brains behind the *Woman on the Wall* prayer ministry and mentorship program, where she's helping women everywhere find their voice and make their mark on the world.

When she's not busy changing lives, you can find Anissa holding down the fort in Virginia, where she's raising two of her seven amazing kids. She's a true powerhouse, balancing family life with her passion for empowering women to be their best selves.

GO FOLLOW ANISSA!

Let's stay connected!

WEBSITE: www.anissadjones.com

INSTAGRAM: @amiteywmofgod

THREADS: @amiteywmofgod

YOUTUBE: @amiteywmofgod

TIK TOK: @amiteywmofgod

www.ingramcontent.com/pod-product-compliance
Lightning Source LLC
Chambersburg PA
CBHW030225170426
43194CB00007BA/863